Sleep, Sheep!

by Marie Powell

amicus readers

Mankato, Minnesota

Ideas for Parents and Teachers

Amicus Readers let children practice reading informational texts at the earliest reading levels. Familiar words and concepts with close photo-text matches support early readers.

Before Reading
- Discuss the cover photo with the child. What does it tell him?
- Ask the child to predict what she will learn in the book.

Read the Book
- "Walk" through the book and look at the photos. Let the child ask questions.
- Read the book to the child, or have the child read independently.

After Reading
- Use the word family list at the end of the book to review the text.
- Prompt the child to make connections. Ask: *What other words end with -eep?*

Amicus Readers are published by Amicus
P.O. Box 1329, Mankato, MN 56002
www.amicuspublishing.us

Copyright © 2014. International copyright reserved in all countries. No part of this book may be reproduced in any form without written permission from the publisher.

Library of Congress Cataloging-in-Publication Data

Powell, Marie, 1958-
 Sleep, sheep! / Marie Powell.
    pages cm. -- (Word families)
 ISBN 978-1-60753-517-1 (hardcover) -- ISBN 978-1-60753-546-1 (eBook)
 1. Reading--Phonetic method. 2. Readers (Primary) I. Title.
 LB1573.3.P696 2013
 372.46'5--dc23

                    2013010399

Photo Credits: Shutterstock Images, cover, 3, 4, 8, 9, 11, 12; Visuell Design/Shutterstock Images, 1; Dejan Gileski/Shutterstock Images, 7; John Carnemolla/Shutterstock Images, 10; Walter Quirtmair/Shutterstock Images, 13; Graeme Dawes/Shutterstock Images, 15

Produced for Amicus by The Peterson Publishing Company and Red Line Editorial.

Editor Jenna Gleisner
Designer Marie Tupy
Printed in the United States of America
Mankato, MN
July, 2013
PA 1938
10 9 8 7 6 5 4 3 2 1

Sheep eat grass on a hill.

The sun is going down.

It is time for the **sheep**

to go home and **sleep**.

4

The **sheep** walk up the **steep** hill. They see a **jeep**.

The **sheep** stop at the pond for a drink. The pond is **deep**.

In the barn, the **sheep** settle down to **sleep**. Their thick wool will **keep** them warm.

9

The **sheep** try to **sleep**.

But the chicks **cheep**

and **peep**. **Peep**! **Peep**!

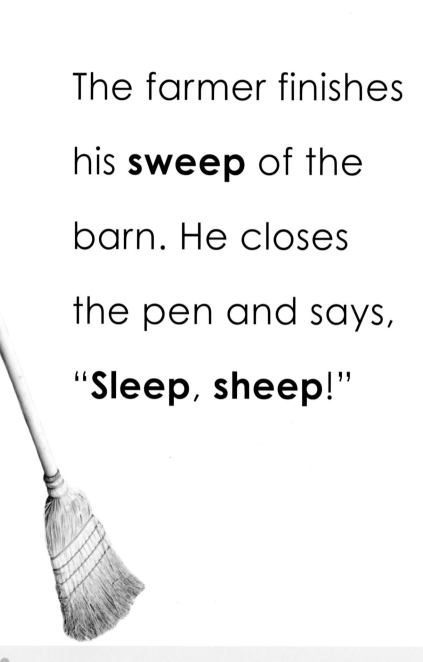

The farmer finishes his **sweep** of the barn. He closes the pen and says, "**Sleep**, **sheep**!"

The **sheep** finally

close their eyes

and fall **asleep**.

Good night, **sheep**!

Word Family: -eep

Word families are groups of words
that rhyme and are spelled the same.

Here are the **-eep** words in this book:

asleep
beep
cheep
deep
jeep
keep
peep
sheep
sleep
steep
sweep

Can you spell any other words
with **-eep**?